ANDY WILLIAMS

CHRISTMAS ❄ COLLECTION

ISBN 978-1-4234-9603-8

HAL•LEONARD®
CORPORATION
7777 W. BLUEMOUND RD. P.O. BOX 13819 MILWAUKEE, WI 53213

Visit Hal Leonard Online at
www.halleonard.com

ANDY WILLIAMS

Andy Williams began his amazing career in his hometown of Wall Lake, Iowa. It was there he started singing with his three brothers in a local Presbyterian church choir established by his parents. At the tender age of 8, Andy made his professional singing debut as part of the Williams Brothers Quartet. The brothers became regulars on radio station WHO's "Iowa's Barn Dance Show" in Des Moines, Iowa. From there the brothers continued to be featured prominently on national stations like WLS in Chicago and WLW in Cincinnati. The widespread radio exposure brought the brothers a considerable following which eventually caught the attention of Bing Crosby. With Crosby, Andy and his brothers made their first professional recording, "Swinging on a Star," which became a tremendous hit in 1944.

In 1947, Andy and his brothers teamed up with comedienne Kay Thompson (author of the popular children's book series *Eloise*) for a successful, trend setting nightclub act. Thompson and the brothers spent the next few years performing all over the U.S. and in London, but it came to an end in 1951 as the group disbanded and each brother went his own way. Andy chose to move to New York to pursue his vocal career.

While in New York, Andy became a regular performer on Steve Allen's *Tonight Show*, which led to his first recording contract with Cadence Records. It wasn't long before Andy had his first Top 10 hit with "Canadian Sunset." A string of hits followed, including "Butterfly," "Lonely Street," "Village of St. Bernadette," and "The Hawaiian Wedding Song," for which he received the first of his five GRAMMY® Award nominations.

His work in television continued with regular guest appearances on the Dinah Shore and Perry Como shows, and in 1958 he presented *The Chevy Showroom with Andy Williams*. In the summer of 1959, Andy was chosen by CBS to host a variety program replacing *The Gary Moore Show* for a thirteen-week period. When this series of shows concluded, Andy began to concentrate on one-hour television specials. The first, "Music from Schubert Alley," was presented by NBC on November 13, 1959.

A change in recording labels kicked Andy's career into high gear when he began his 25-year association with Columbia Records in 1962. Almost immediately he scored his first Top 10 hit for Columbia, "Can't Get Used to Losing You." Many more hits followed, but none would become more associated with Andy Williams than "Moon River," the Oscar winning song from the film *Breakfast at Tiffany's*. This song became his theme song and propelled the album, *Moon River and Other Great Movie Themes* to the top of the charts. The following year Andy released the album *Days of Wine and Roses*, which spent an incredible sixteen weeks at #1 and stayed on the charts for over 100 weeks. His subsequent recordings were best sellers and resulted in eighteen gold and three platinum-certified albums.

Williams became a superstar after the debut of his weekly television series on NBC, *The Andy Williams Show*. His new variety show was seen for the first time on September 16, 1962, and ran for nine years, winning three Emmy Awards for Best Musical/Variety Series (1966, 1967, and 1969). It was one of NBC's top rated programs, and helped launch his classic Christmas specials featuring the entire Williams family.

Live performances continued to be a big part of Andy's career, and in 1966 he opened at Caesar's Palace and subsequently headlined at the famed Las Vegas hotel for the next twenty years. By the time *The Andy Williams Show* ended in 1972, Andy had become a true international superstar. With tremendous world-wide record sales and global distribution of his television show, he is just as popular in other countries as he is in the United States. This recognition prompted several tours of England, Europe, Australia, Japan, and Asia, breaking attendance records wherever he appeared. Andy currently performs at the Andy Williams Moon River Theater in Branson, Missouri, where he continues to present his live Variety and award-winning Christmas shows.

BLUE CHRISTMAS

Words and Music by BILLY HAYES
and JAY JOHNSON

blue ____ Christ - mas.

Instrumental solo

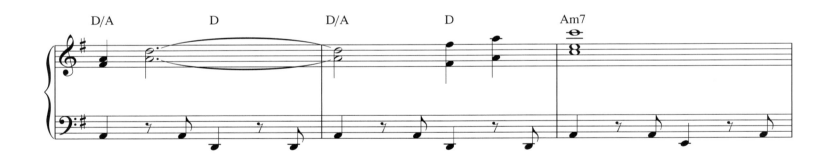

Solo ends Dec - o - ra -

THE BELLS OF ST. MARY'S

Traditional
Words by DOUGLAS FURBER
Music by A. EMMETT ADAMS

CHRISTMAS BELLS

Traditional
Words and Music by MYKOLA DMYTROVYCH LEONTOVYCH
and MINNA LOUISE HOHMAN

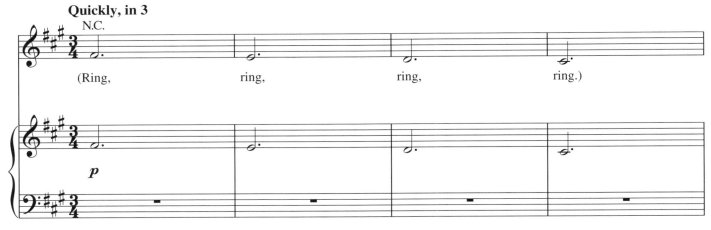

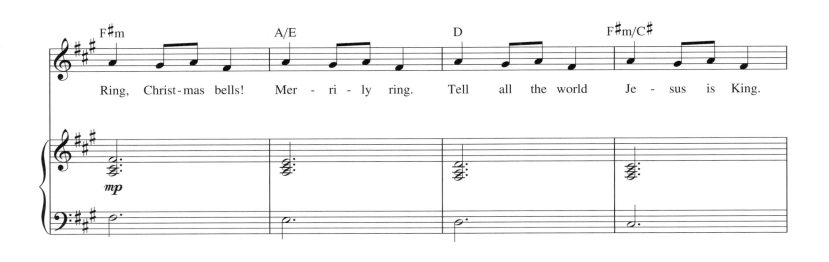

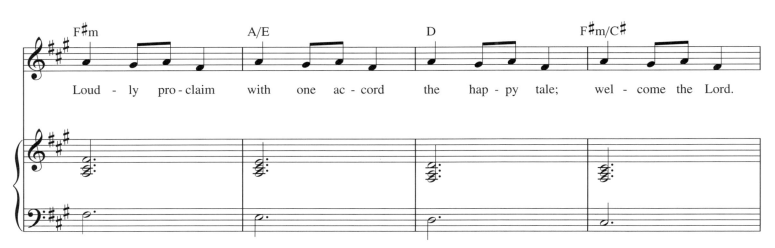

THE CHRISTMAS SONG
(Chestnuts Roasting on an Open Fire)

Music and Lyric by MEL TORMÉ
and ROBERT WELLS

DO YOU HEAR WHAT I HEAR

Words and Music by NOEL REGNEY
and GLORIA SHAYNE

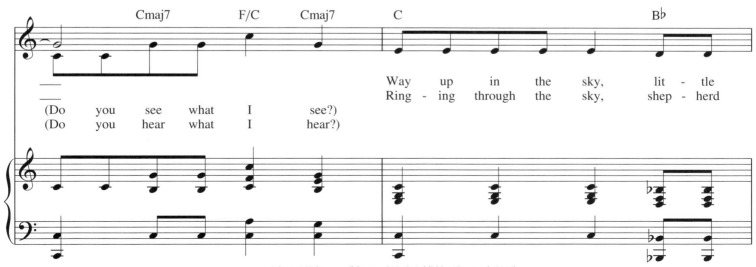

THE FIRST NOEL

Traditional

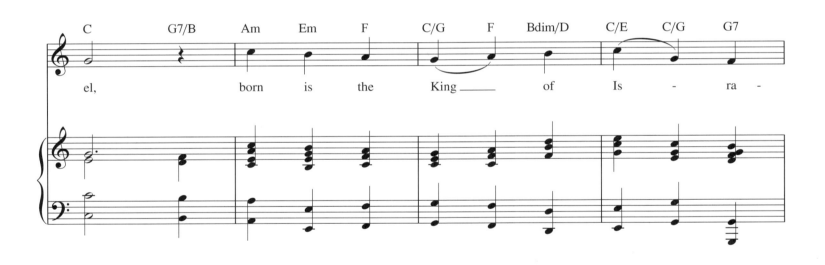

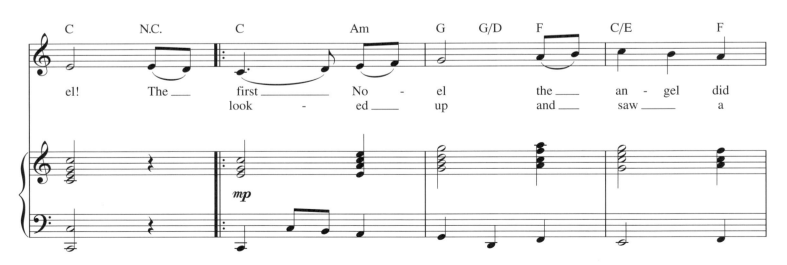

HAPPY HOLIDAY / THE HOLIDAY SEASON

HAPPY HOLIDAY
from the Motion Picture Irving Berlin's HOLIDAY INN
Words and Music by IRVING BERLIN

THE HOLIDAY SEASON

Words and Music by KAY THOMPSON

(Lyrics, verse 1 / verse 2):

Hol - i - day!) (Hap - py Hol - i - day!) It's the

hol - i - day sea - son, _____ and San - ta Claus _ is
hol - i - day sea - son, _____ and San - ta Claus _ has

com - in' 'round, _ the Christ - mas snow is white on the ground. _
got a toy _ for ev - 'ry good girl and good lit - tle boy. _

When old San - ta gets in - to town, _ he'll be com - in' down the chim - ney, down. _
San - ta's a great big bun - dle of joy _ when he's com - in' down the chim - ney, down. _

I'LL BE HOME FOR CHRISTMAS

Words and Music by KIM GANNON
and WALTER KENT

MY FAVORITE THINGS
from THE SOUND OF MUSIC

Lyrics by OSCAR HAMMERSTEIN II
Music by RICHARD RODGERS

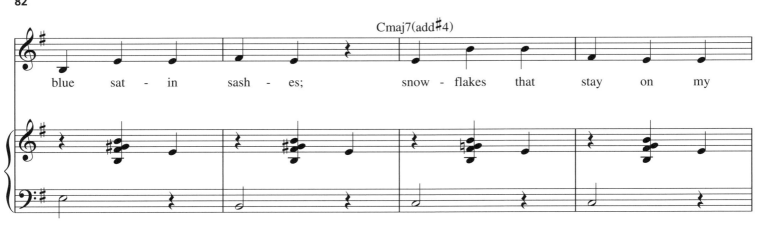

blue sat - in sash - es; snow - flakes that stay on my

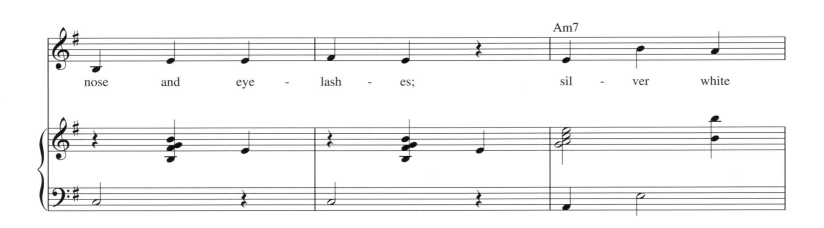

nose and eye - lash - es; sil - ver white

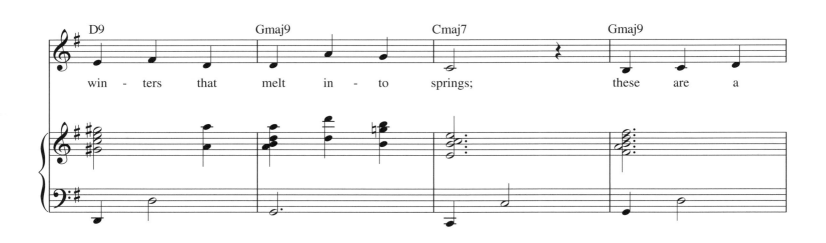

win - ters that melt in - to springs; these are a

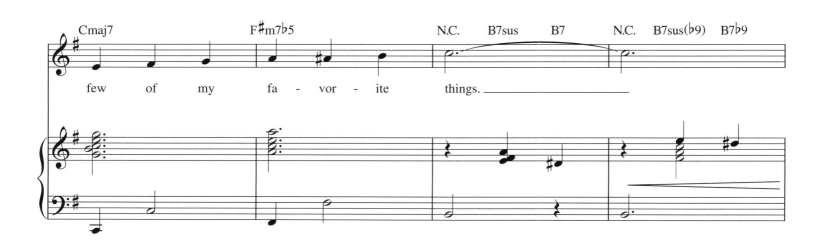

few of my fa - vor - ite things.

things _____ and then I don't

feel _____ so bad. _____

SILVER BELLS

from the Paramount Picture THE LEMON DROP KID

Words and Music by JAY LIVINGSTON
and RAY EVANS

WHITE CHRISTMAS

from the Motion Picture Irving Berlin's HOLIDAY INN

Words and Music by
IRVING BERLIN

SLEIGH RIDE

Music by LEROY ANDERSON
Words by MITCHELL PARISH

Moderate Samba

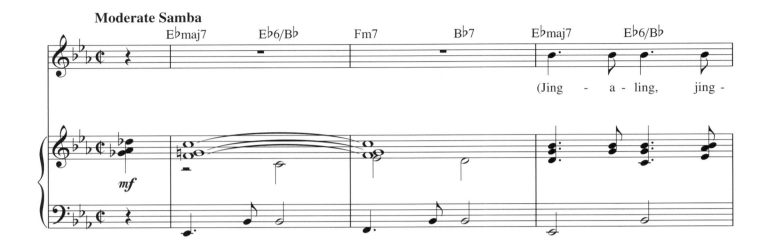

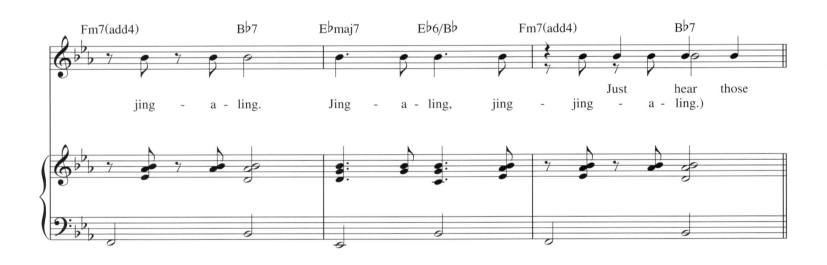

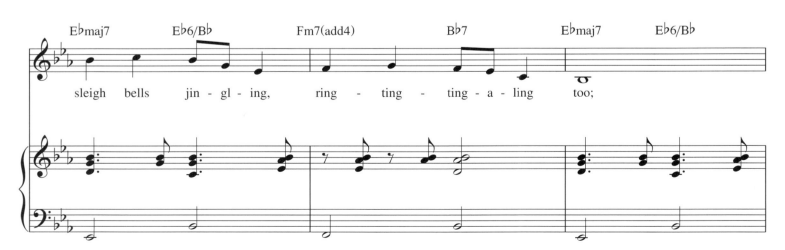

VILLAGE OF ST. BERNADETTE

Words and Music by
EULA PARKER

WHAT ARE YOU DOING NEW YEAR'S EVE?

By FRANK LOESSER

WINTER WONDERLAND

Words by DICK SMITH
Music by FELIX BERNARD

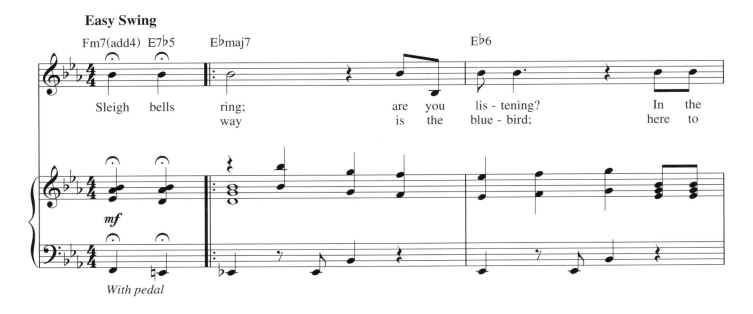